Living Your Desired LIFE

Dr. Malcolm Burton

Living Your Desired Life

Copyright © 2018 by Dr. Malcolm Burton

All rights reserved. No part of this book may be reproduced or transmitted in any form or by any means without written permission of the author.

ISBN-13: 978-1-7324922-2-6

Printed in the United States of America

RevMedia Publishing

PO BOX 5172, Kingwood, TX 77325

No part of this book may be reproduced or transmitted in any form or by any means, electronic or mechanical—including photocopying, recording, or by any information storage and retrieval system—without permission in writing from the publisher.

Contents

Why I Wrote This Book 5
1. Honor The Lord 7
2. Put God First 9
3. Pursue Your God Dream 11
4. Master The Power of Focus 13
5. Unleash The Force of Honor 15
6. Pray in The Spirit 17
7. Make Bold Declarations of Faith 21
8. See Yourself as Something Greater 23
9. Embrace The Jesus Lifestyle 25
10. Celebrate Your Mentor 29
11. Three Steps To Sustained Success 33
12. Live Without Shame 37
13. Right Words Shake Up Your Enemy 39
14. I Am Saved 41
15. My Faith Confession 43
16. Learning Facts 45
17. His Word 47
18. Learning From a Communist 49
19. Destined To...Last 51
20. Consider The Consequences 53
21. Unintended Consequence 55
22. More Awful News 57
23. Three Thoughts About Words 59
24. Silencing The Haters 61
25. Thoughts on Destiny 63
26. My First Valentine 65
27. You Can't Advance Beyond Your Faith 67
28. An Early Church Miracle 69
29. I Hate Religion 71
30. I Don't Want to Forget 73
31. Prospecting 75

Why I Wrote This Book

My Choices Were Limited.

I grew up in rural East Texas.

Our region is called *"The Big Thicket"*.

It is even more bio diverse than the Amazon Basin.

The East Fork of The San Jacinto River crossed our property.

There only seemed to be a few choices for work: be a logger, work as a driller in the oilfield, do carpentry, or be in oilfield construction.

The old ways were passing quickly.

Gus "Paw Paw" Burton was a cattle rancher.

Frederick "Papa Blum", my maternal grandfather, trapped fur.

Nothing in me wanted to do any of that sort of work.

Even when I was young I remember standing on the river bridge.

As I looked at the waters flowing below I dreamed of a life in writing or ministry. The flow seemed to speak to me there are more options than we routinely see around us.

If this describes you, find your own river.

Deliberately ponder the plan of God for your life.

Stand quietly and look at the flow as you think big thoughts.

Consider the general principles in this book as you think of *Living Your Desired Life.*

This book contains 31 general principles, things you can do and ways to think, that you can employ to generate the kind of life you desire to live.

Having God's best is completely possible.

It requires a dream...*and enough faith to act on your dream.*

I look forward to hearing your success story.

Malcolm Burton
June, 2018
Madison County, Texas

1
Honor The Lord

Humility Produces Honor.

Honor produces inestimably good results.

We serve a great God who passionately loves us.

His thoughts, intentions and deeds only involve good things.

The only way I "fear the Lord" is in regard to displeasing Him. I do not live in fear of Divine Retribution.

I am one of His children. My children have never lived in fear of Dad's retribution because striking back is not in my nature.

In a Christian context, "fear" is not a slavish emotion linked to a sense of impending doom. It is simply the emotional desire not to disrespect God.

In this life we reap what we sow.

Humility is recognizing the greatness of another.

No one and nothing is greater than the Lord our God.

I reap honor as I humbly sow respect into my relationship with God.

> "The reward of humility is the fear of the Lord, along with wealth, honor, and life," (Proverbs 22:4 ISV).

2
Put God First

Impossible.

Every Christian desires to put God first.

In the flesh this is a complete impossibility.

For the Christian this is not just possible, but imperative.

Such a fruitful life cannot be lived without being Born Again.

Our old nature desires only to please ourselves. Our body screams for pleasure. Our mind constantly craves the freedom to wander and entertain every kind of thought.

The answer is proper priorities which produce a lifestyle that constantly solicits and uses the opinions of God.

We are Ambassadors for Christ.

Jesus makes His appeal through us.

Your life of victory will draw others into reconciliation with God and man.

Say this aloud, "The new life is my life. I am reconciled to God and man."

> *"Therefore, if anyone is iin Christ, he is a new creation. The old has passed away; behold, the new has come. 18 All this is from God, who through Christ reconciled us to*

himself and gave us the ministry of reconciliation; 19 that is, in Christ God was reconciling the world to himself, not counting their trespasses against them, and entrusting to us the message of reconciliation. 20 Therefore, we are ambassadors for Christ, God making his appeal through us. We implore you on behalf of Christ, be reconciled to God. 21 For our sake he made him to be sin who knew no sin, so that in him we might become the righteousness of God," (2 Corinthians 5:17-21, ESV).

3
Pursue Your God Dream

Intimidation.

Destiny can be intimidating.

Your destiny hinges upon pursuing your dream.

God gives us a dream. Obstacles are then arrayed against our dream.

God does not give us a dream in order to frustrate, irritate or discourage us.

God gives us a dream to energize toward fulfilling His will for our life,

We must understand obstacles originate in hell.

Our answers exist in the Holy Spirit realm. We must expect Him to speak.

Joshua knew his destiny was to lead Israel after Moses died. Even so, hell had apparently arrayed "mind games" against him.

Scripture reveals Joshua as having lived an exemplary life of success. He, just like we, had the promises of God.

> "Moses My servant is dead. Now therefore, arise, go over this Jordan, you and all this people, to the land which I am giving to them—the children of Israel. 3 Every place that the sole of your foot will tread upon I have given you, as I said

> to Moses. *4 From the wilderness and this Lebanon as far as the great river, the River Euphrates, all the land of the Hittites, and to the Great Sea toward the going down of the sun, shall be your territory. 5 No man shall be able to stand before you all the days of your life; as I was with Moses, so I will be with you. I will not leave you nor forsake you,"* (Joshua 1:2-5, NKJV).

God always goes the extra mile.

He did so with Joshua by giving him an extra boost.

> *"Be strong and of good courage; do not be afraid, nor be dismayed, for the Lord your God is with you wherever you go,"* (1:9).

Refuse dismay today.

Refuse dismay every day.

Instead, *"Be Strong and Courageous..."*

4
Master The Power of Focus

Eyeglasses.

I don't like them. But I do wear them. I wear them for a reason. They are necessary to my focus. Without eyeglasses words are a scrambled mess,

Without the help of the Holy Spirit the world looks like a scrambled mess.

My living space is one of competition. Moment by moment I find myself fighting with an array of things that, both rightly and wrongly, desire my focus.

Three Areas of Chosen Focus

1. The Word of God. *"I have inclined my heart to perform Your statutes forever, to the very end," (Psalm 119:112, NKJV).*

2. The Jesus Lifestyle. *"Fixing our eyes on Jesus, the pioneer and perfecter of faith," (Hebrews 12:2).*

3. The Moment By Moment Necessity of Grace. *"Therefore guard your minds, be sober, and hope to the end for the grace that is to be brought to you at the revelation of Jesus Christ," (1 Peter 1:13).*

Life is filled with challenges.

We can defeat every challenge through focus.

Choose to keep your focus with the help of the Word and the Holy Spirit.

> *"Those who focus upon Him are radiant; their faces are never covered with shame,"*
> *(Psalm 34:5, Author's Personal Interpretation).*

5
Unleash The Force of Honor

Honor Is A Force.

Honor is more than a principle.

Honor is a power source for righteous living.

It is obvious that we should honor the Lord, but the force of honor extends beyond there.

Facts About Honor

We always need the power of God working for us.

Giving honor where it is due releases tremendous power,

As we honor others, the Holy Spirit releases the force of honor to work for us.

Three Groups Worthy of Honor

1. Honor Your Parents *"Honor your father and your mother, so that you may live long in the land the Lord your God is giving you. (Exodus 20:12).*

2. Honor Civilian Authorities *"...give to everyone what you owe them: If you owe taxes, pay taxes; if revenue, then revenue; if respect, then respect; if honor, then honor," (Romans 13:7).*

3. Honor Church Leaders *"The elders who direct the affairs of the church well are worthy of double honor, especially those whose* work is preaching and teaching," (1 Timothy 5:17).

Try to "out do" others in demonstrating honor today.

Make it your personal goal to demonstrate honor to those you interact with on a daily basis.

6
Pray in The Spirit

Tongues.

Tongues is an often misunderstood gift.

It is also a commonly underutilized spiritual gift.

Five Ways Praying in Tongues Improves Your Life

1. Praying in Tongues Causes Mysteries to Be Revealed

> "For he who speaks in a tongue does not speak to men but to God, for no one understands him; however, in the spirit he speaks mysteries," (1 Cor. 14:2, NKJV).

Mysterion is the Greek word for mystery. It means "Truth that is hidden until God chooses to reveal it."

As we are in intimate conversation with God by praying in the Spirit, we find our understanding of mysteries is increasing.

I've noticed that many of the things I've come to recognize while praying in the Spirit do not necessarily come by the sequence of questions and answers. My best explanation is I simply come out of the prayer time understanding things I'd not known prior to then.

2. Praying in Tongues Unlocks Other Spiritual Gifts

> "For to one is given the word of wisdom through the Spirit, to another the word of knowledge through the same Spirit

> ... *to another prophecy, to another discerning of spirits, to another different kinds of tongues, to another the interpretation of tongues," (1 Corinthians 12:8; 10).*

These gifts work in times apart from prayer. However, prayer seems to condition the atmosphere for them to operate more effectively.

3. Praying in Tongues Causes The Bible to Come Alive

> *"However, when He, the Spirit of truth, has come, He will guide you into all truth; for He will not speak on His own authority, but whatever He hears He will speak," (John 16:13).*

Jesus ascended back to heaven. The Holy Spirit came to earth and remained. Jesus, as the Word of God made flesh, is no longer on earth.

The Holy Spirit, The Revealer, gives us insight into all things pertaining to Jesus. As Jesus was The Word of God in human form, He is the personification of all things written and spoken as the Word. in the flesh.

He is therefore, the totality of all wisdom. As we pray in the Spirit our insight of who He is becomes revealed to us.

4. Praying in Tongues Connects Us Directly to God

> *"For he who speaks in a tongue does not speak to men but to God..." (1 Corinthians 14:2).*

Here Paul is referring to the devotional tongue.

At the time of Spirit-Baptism each believer is given a "prayer language." This could correctly be referred to as our "devotional tongue" and its highest and best use is during times of personal intercession and interaction with The Lord. There is a difference between this devotional tongue and the ministry tongue that is ministered publicly and requires interpretation.

In our prayer language we are speaking directly to God. No interpretation is required as the Holy Spirit knows all things. Master using your prayer language. No other being (human, angelic, or demonic) can understand this flow of prayer and worship you are offering to God.

5. Praying in Tongues Will Change Your Perspective on Spiritual Warfare

"Praying always with all prayer and supplication in the Spirit," (Eph. 6:18).

Spiritual warfare is often misunderstood. It is represented by many as a time of intense struggle. Some believe it is only available to those called to intercession. This is simply inaccurate. Note there that Paul is encouraging all believers to use tongues as a form of warfare.

It is my belief that demonic powers are driven back each time I pray in the Holy Spirit. When I'm in this mode I pray until I sense change. It is also my belief that doors of opportunity are opened when I pray in the Holy Spirit. Paul explains this in Romans.

Even when I don't know what to pray, the Holy Spirit does.

"And the Holy Spirit helps us in our weakness. For example, we don't know what God wants us to pray for. But the Holy Spirit prays for us with groanings that cannot be expressed in words," (Romans 8:26, NLT).

7
Make Bold Declarations of Faith

Drought Is Devastating.

I live in farm and ranch country.

I'm very well familiar with the power of drought. The rising price of food is an initial sign of drought. City managers begin scrambling for water sources as rivers dry up.

Spiritual drought is equally devastating. During such times we lose our ability to "see by faith." If we are not careful we will lose control of our tongue and begin speaking death.

The prophet Elijah was in a conflict with the Israeli King Ahab.

Ahab's disobedience and bold worship of pagan gods had brought a curse upon the entire region. Water sources were drying up. Farmers were seeing only a limited amount of produce from their crops.

As Elijah confronted Ahab on Mount Carmel, he heard something in the spirit realm. What he heard gave him the confidence to speak, "Then Elijah said to Ahab, "Go up, eat and drink; for there is the sound of abundance of rain."

Why do we make such declarations? We have the spirit of faith.

> "And since we have the same spirit of faith, according to what is written, "I believed and therefore I spoke," we also believe and therefore speak," (2 Corinthians 4:13).

The Book of Job is the oldest collection of scriptures. Job declared,

> "You will also declare a thing, and it will be established for you," (Job 22:28).

Not only should we be diligent to pray, we should make bold declarations.

State, like Elijah, what you believe is about to happen. "Rain! Get ready for rain! Rain is coming!" Elijah shouted in the face of Ahab.

Yet, the rain did not immediately come. Elijah was undeterred. He kept speaking his faith. As he kept speaking, he looked for confirmation of rain.

He sent his assistant outside to look for clouds forming over the ocean. Six times the man saw nothing. On the seventh time the servant returned he said, "I see a cloud the size of a man's hand."

Elijah made a bold declaration: "Go up, say to Ahab, 'Prepare *your chariot*, and go down before the rain stops you.'"

We all have drought situations. Use your faith and speak boldly to your drought. Declare, "My situation is changing. The drought is ending. The rain of the Holy Spirit is at hand. A season of plenty is mine today."

Your faith will cause your river to flow.

Things will turn around!

Declare it today!

8
See Yourself as Something Greater

I Love My Uncle.

He is a truly great man.

He led a local congregation to success.

Under his leadership they were able to do something exceptional. The church had owned real estate in a prime location for years, but no progress had been made toward relocation.

Pastor Harold Blum, who has been married to Norine Blum for over 50 years, led the congregation in erecting a lovely building on the property that had been fallow for so many years.

During the funeral of our cousin, Mellie, Coleman, he spoke what I found to be life changing words.

"Mellie was an unusual lady. She was a professional musician who owned her own business when few women did such a thing. Mellie had contracts to play piano or organ for several funeral homes in our region. She taught private music lessons. During a time when many women were made to feel like they were something less, she saw herself as something more."

Uncle Harold then told a story something that happened on a trip. He was in the San Juan Mountains of Colorado near Wolf Creek. A sign marked a spot as the Continental Divide.

"It was snowing lightly, and as I straddled the line facing

south I knew that the snow that fell to earth to the west would eventually travel into the Pacific Ocean. Most of the snow falling to the east would someday melt and reach the waters of the Gulf of Mexico, which is only about 75 miles from my home."

"Each bit of rain or snow will eventually become part of something greater than they were when they fell to earth."

"Sister Mellie saw herself as part of something greater and refused to be limited by the prejudiced opinions of people."

People will limit you.

Some will do so by design.

God always desires to increase us.

By His very nature God desires to release more into us.

He proved this from the start, "God said, 'Let us make man in our image, after our likeness. And let them have dominion over the fish of the sea and over the birds of the heavens and over the livestock and over all the earth and over every creeping thing that creeps on the earth,'" (Genesis 1:26).

Refuse a poor self-image. Instead, see yourself as more. Jesus has never made anyone less. By the power of relationship, He always makes us more.

See your life as flowing out to be part of something far greater.

9
Embrace The Jesus Lifestyle

Humanity Is Obsessed With Lifestyle.

Advice of how to live is constantly flowing to us.

What to wear, what to drive, how to eat and what to drive.

We are bombarded with unsolicited information on how to live.

By choosing this book you have demonstrated a desire for insight. In 2 Corinthians 5:17 we read

> "Therefore, if anyone is in Christ, he is a new creation. The old has passed away; behold, the new has come."

Being born again means exactly that: we begin to live a new life. When we fully embrace the Jesus Lifestyle we find ourselves being completely transformed.

Deliberately Try To Please The Lord

If you are debating yourself about whether or not something is okay, stop immediately and move away. If a decision requires so much internal debate on the issue of something being right or wrong, get away immediately.

Consciously Live a Life of Prayer

> "Pray without ceasing," (1 Thessalonians 5:17).

Prayer is not always sitting alone in a room with your eyes

closed and your hands extended. Prayer is as simple as reaching out to God in faith. When you are constantly engaged in an internal dialogue with God you can rest assured your life is quite likely pleasing to Him. This constant dialogue with God is proof of how much He matters in your life.

Think of Yourself as a Market Place Minister

We are not all called to the five-fold preaching ministry. We are, however all called to ministry. Paul explains in 2 Corinthians 5:18,

> "All this is from God, who through Christ reconciled us to himself and gave us the ministry of reconciliation;" (ESV).

One of the most effective ministers I've known has never preached a sermon. However, it is clear to me she does the work of the ministry in her work place. Literally hundreds have been born again, and an even larger number of backsliders have been restored through her loving ministry of grace.

My cousin, The Rev. Mr. Larry Fussell, a bi-vocational minister in the United Methodist Church, has seen far greater results in the work place than he has seen in the pulpit. For several years he has taken an troop of Christian actors to a local nursing home. As I write this over 1200 seniors have come to know Jesus. One 88-year-old had lived her entire life in the United States without having heard the plan of salvation until Larry saw the nursing home as more than a business client.

Position Yourself As Part of the Church, The Body of Christ

The church is not a building, but a group of believers who are building their lives upon their faith in the Word of God.

Your faith will increase as you interact with other believers. You will find your faith sharpened by the testimonies of others.

Little if anything is more important to Christianity than being part of a local church. As you're around other believers you will find Proverbs 27:17 to be true as,

> *"Iron sharpens iron, and one man sharpens another" (ESV)*

10
Celebrate Your Mentor

Mentoring Is Vital.

We must have a Mentor.
We must learn to be a Mentor.
A Mentor is an experienced, trusted advisor.

My Mother Was My First Mentor

"Train up a child in the way he should go, and even when he is old he will not depart from it," (Proverbs 22:6)

Mama taught me how to read. That would have been enough, but she did more. Mom instilled in me an intense desire to please God. She drilled into me the necessity of seeing the best in others. Mom demonstrated the essential need for honesty in all relationships. Mom proved to me it is possible to walk with God throughout my lifetime.

Effective Friendships Involve Mentoring

"As iron sharpens iron, so one man sharpens another," (Proverbs 27:17).

Pastor Harold Herring is a loyal friend. When I spend time around him I get better. He constantly challenges me to learn more and demonstrate it. Harold gave me words to live by, "If you're the smartest person in your circle of friends, you need some new friends."

Believers Should Have a Paul, a Barnabas and a Timothy

> *"Having so fond an affection for you, we were well-pleased to impart to you not only the gospel of God, but also our own lives, because you had become very dear to us," (1 Thessalonians 2:8).*

We need a Paul. Someone who knows more. We need a Barnabas. Paul and Barnabas were equals. We need a Timothy. We need someone we can impart to. By reaching, fellowship, and giving out we complete the cycle. Recently, I realized I do not have a "Paul" in my life. My lifelong Mentor died several years ago. In my grief I knew he was irreplaceable. However, the role he played must be filed by someone.

The Holy Spirit is the Ultimate Mentor

> *"But the helper, the Holy Spirit, Whom the Father will send in My name, He will teach you all things and bring to your remembrance all I said to you," (John 14:26).*

He knows everything. Yes, He knows everyone. He understands your likes and dislikes. He knows your strengths and your weaknesses. He is the most gracious individual you will ever meet. He is the only person on earth you can please 100% of the time. How can this be? He will not judge you based upon what He sees, but what He knows. He is the only one who knows the intention of your heart, and has the ability to lead you in the direction that is best for you and everyone around you.

During crisis times when you don't really know what to say, He is the one who fills your mouth with the right words.

Pay Close Attention to the Lives of Those You Mentor

> *"Know well the condition of your flocks. And pay attention*

to your herds," (Proverbs 27:23).

Dr. Ron Smith was my spiritual father. He was also a mentor who had no peers. Yes, our relationship was intensely a spiritual one. However, he was also knowledgeable about my finances, and my family. Simply put, he gave sharp attention to every area of my life. The greatest gift he gave me was access. And, I will be thankful for that access.

11
Three Steps To Sustained Success

Success.

We all want success. We will find varying degrees. Yet, we can't keep it until we define it. Success is the accomplishment of an aim or purpose. For most of us success involves living in a state of financial security.

King David obviously believed the pathway of blessing involved pleasing God.

> *"And keep the charge of the Lord your God: to walk in His ways, to keep His statutes, His commandments, His judgments, and His testimonies, as it is written in the Law of Moses, that you may prosper in all that you do and wherever you turn;" (1 Kings 2:3).*

Govern Your Thought Life By The Word Of God

Thought Precedes Action.

Everything begins with a thought. Keep your focus on the good things.

> *"Finally brethren, whatever things are true, whatever things are noble, whatever things are just, whatever things are pure, whatever things are lovely, whatever things are of god report, if there is virtue, and if there is anything praiseworthy---meditate upon these things," (Philippians 4:8).*

What you think the longest becomes the strongest.

The husband of a friend died. The wife was left with four daughters. Almost all the money they had amassed was wrapped up in a new house they were finishing. During the last week of work a couple approached my friend and asked her if the house was for sale. They made an offer that was too much for her to turn down.

My friend immediately bought a house where she and her daughters could live. She also felt God had revealed a pathway to her future success by building and "flipping" homes. Today her daughters are all happily married, and my friend lives a secure lifestyle in the Cascade Mountains of California.

Think in Terms of Opportunity

Making money was not my challenge. I can honestly say I have been gifted to make money. Dennis, my younger brother is better. He sees money everywhere. How? He doesn't ignore any chance to make money. He understands and maximizes the law of opportunity.

As we recently drove down the road together I commented about a huge tractor tire in the front yard of a country home. He turned around, drove back to look at the tire. The owner came outside and he negotiated the owner from a price of $300 to $150 cash.

Dennis then called someone and asked, "Do you still need that tractor tire we spoke about?" He sold the tire to a tractor operator for $750. Dennis made $600 by seeing and acting upon an opportunity.

Quickly Obey God and Turn What You Have Into More

A friend lived in Denver. He pastored a strong church there. While he was not wealthy, he was doing well. While driving down the interstate he heard God speak.

"Purchase that plot of land on the right side of the highway."

He pulled over, walked back and found a sign lying flat in the ditch. He called the phone number and told the owner was asking an unbelievably low price of $20,000 cash for the 20-acre parcel. He called his wife, and told her what He had heard. She agreed and they acted. The $20,000 withdrawal emptied their family savings account.

Within a month someone called to say they wanted to buy the land. They were only willing to pay $600,000. My friend pushed back and asked for $800,000. The purchaser quickly agreed and the deal was completed in just a few days.

God wants us to prosper.

Please seriously consider this thought.

Our Lord wants us to prosper more than we want to prosper.

12
Live Without Shame

Shame Is Satanic.

Shame has touched everyone. There are things we should regret. Yet, we cannot allow guilt to bind us. Jesus killed the predecessor of shame, guilt. I have sincere regrets, but false guilt? No thanks.

I don't enjoy my physical appearance, but I refuse shame.

A former mentor once said, "Let go of that body image shame. You're never gonna turn a bulldog into a greyhound." Wise man.

I find it particularly painful that I have disappointed people during my lifetime, but I cannot let that truth dominate me to the point I'm made ineffective for those who are in my life today.

Yes, we've all fought shame issues.

But I pray you are, as I am, free today.

One thing has never brought false guilt my way.

> *I can truthfully say, "I am not ashamed of the gospel, for it is the power of God for salvation to everyone who believes," (Romans 1:16).*

Sharing the gospel frees. It frees both the sharer and the recipient.

Paul had plenty of things of which to be ashamed.

However, he had embraced the ultimate shame removing agent: the Holy Spirit. The Holy Spirit depositing the truth of the Word of God deep within his spirit was Paul's antidote.

Conclusion: He was a new creation.

He had embraced freedom in fullness.

False guilt is rampant. Shame binds far too many. If guilt is removed at repentance, shame must go, too.

Enforcing the victory is our choice to make.

I choose to live in Our Lord's freedom.

Please join me by living here...

In The Shame Free Zone.

13
Right Words Shake Up Your Enemy

You Are Progressing.

You're doing better than you know. Every step forward in faith disturbs the demonic realm.

> *"In battle, if you make your opponent flinch, you have already won,"* —Mayamoto Muyashi.

I'm so thankful for the faith message. This belief system brought Christianity alive for me. This systematic approach built my confidence in God's Word.

> *"You say you have faith...Good for you! Demons believe this, and they tremble in terror," (James 2:19 NLT).*

What are You Saying?

Keep speaking your faith. Hell flinches each time you speak. Your words are shaking up the status quo. You're creating the lifestyle your heart desires. Your enemy has flinched. His days are numbered.

Your best days are still ahead of you. Believe it. Say it.

Three Truths About Words

1. Speak Softly to People

> *"A soft answer turns away wrath, but a harsh word stirs up anger," (Proverbs 15:1, ESV).*

People are impacted by what you say. Remember the words of Granny Blum: "Keep your words soft and sweet. They may be the next thing you get to eat."

2. Back Up Your Words With Corresponding Action

> *"But be doers of the word, and not hearers only, deceiving yourselves," (James 1:22 ESV).*

Religious people talk. Genuinely spiritual people "do".

3. On Some Occasions The Best Thing You Can Say Is Nothing

> *"Whoever belittles his neighbor lacks sense, but a man of understanding remains silent. (Proverbs 11:12).*

Belittling speech is trap for the speaker. Proverbs 6:2 says,

> *"You are snared by the words of your mouth; You are taken by the words of your mouth. "*

The evil words you speak against others will boomerang around back at the unwise speaker. When we learn the power of words we are more inclined to remain silent.

14
I Am Saved

I don't feel saved. I feel like a big pile of nothing. The good news is I'm ruled by faith. Faith speaks desires rather than emotions. My faith is intact and speaking the Word of God.

"Whoever" means anyone, without distinction between Jew or Greek. For all have the same Lord, whose boundless resources are available to all who turn to him in faith. For:

> 'Whoever calls upon the name of the Lord shall be saved'.
> (Romans 10:12-13 JB Phillips Translation of The New Testament).

I have called upon the Name of Jesus. The power of the saving Name is at work inside me. This interior work is also producing visible changes on the outside. I'm saved from my past, saved in this moment, and will be saved in my future.

It all started when I called upon the Name of Jesus. My life stays on course by praying in That Name. Whosoever will may still come to Him this day. That thought launched this day with a grin.

I plan to smile all day.

15
My Faith Confession

I'm in His Will.

I'm in His will for my life. I'm in His will for my ministry. The things I've asked for are coming to pass. How do I know? I've asked for things He offers.

> "This is the confidence we have before Him, that, if we ask anything according to His will, He hears us," (1 John 5:14).

The Bible is filled with promises. Promises for a good future filled with hope.

> The Holy Spirit spoke through the Prophet Jeremiah, "For I know the thoughts that I think toward you, says the Lord, thoughts of peace and not of evil, to give you a future and a hope," (Jeremiah 29:11).

I deliberately claim those promises as mine today.

My spirit is eternally cleansed. My mind is clear and renewed by faith in God's Word. My body will serve me as I live out my call to ministry.

Ephesians 3:12 is my focus. I am living in eternal purpose. I will approach Jesus in bold faith.

> "...in whom we have boldness and access."

I will experience supernatural success today. This success is produces by spiritual boldness. I will be boldly confident because He has given me access. These are the things I'm saying about my life today. Words create a climate for success or failure. What are you saying about your life?

16
Learning Facts

The Easy Way Is Pleasant.

The Hard Way is unforgettable.

College Memories

I had little in common with my college peers. I came from rural Texas, and they were "Preppies". At best my family was Middle Class, while they were moneyed.

I Preferred Watching

Observation is less risky than interaction. Yet, some degree of interaction is inevitable. I did not expect to be embraced... *and I wasn't.* My only desire was to demonstrate my academic excellence. There was no real danger in watching those around me so long as I had no real involvement.

I Learned A Hard Lesson

I did become involved with a few. Honestly, the involvement was not for my good. I learned, "People make me better, or they make me worse." The negative education continued, "Those who do not increase my life will inevitably decrease me.

Conclusion: I am no more effective than my weakest relationship.

17
His Word

The Bible.

The Logos of God. No greater book has been written. No greater book will ever be written. My entire life has been changed by this one book.

I woke up this morning "seeing" revival in Asia. How? The supernatural claims of The Bible.

> *"God says, In the last days I will pour out My Spirit upon all kinds of people. Your sons and daughters will prophesy. Your young men will see visions, and your old men shall dream dreams," (Acts 2:17 New Century Version).*

My faith has been stirred by the supernatural claims of The Bible. My heart goes out to those who believe such things are past. They are missing out on great events. At a time when most of my friends are thinking of retirement, I'm gearing up. Why? The Holy Spirit and my faith stirs The Word I've chosen to plant inside myself.

The supernatural claims of The Bible get me out of bed. The supernatural claims of The Bible stoke my imagination. The supernatural claims of The Bible cause me to see a good future.

Jesus gives an insight in Luke 19:13,

> *"So he called ten of his servants, delivered to them ten minas, and said to them, 'Do business till I come.'"*

We are not supposed to be wringing our hands and crying. No, we are to reign. Put another way, " Do business until I come." What business is this? His business! It begins with, is sustained and concluded by His Word.

My faith is visionary because I have received His Living Word. His Holy Spirit is energizing my faith again this day. My faith is rising and my doubts are diminishing. I deliberately "see" better things... by faith.

I'm driven by choosing the supernatural. I'm thinking and believing His thoughts. The days ahead really will be better.

Make the choice with me.

Let's "go there!"

18
Learning From a Communist

Bertold Brecht.

He was a Communist playwright/director. He fled Germany because he feared Adolf Hitler. From the U.S. he wrote magazine articles that tormented Nazis. When Germany was in full retreat he wrote, "To those fleeing the Russian onslaught, there is no longer a road home."

I had a really tough day. The loneliness bug bit me. I spent the day thinking of Mom. I'm better today because I've chosen my focus. Even during rough periods I'll decide to embrace "better".

Brecht's taunt, or one like it, will never work against me. There is still a road home for me. I walk it daily.

It gets brighter each day (Proverbs 4:18).

I'm smiling.

Hope you are.

19
Destined To...Last

They tied for last. They attended a prestigious school. Both graduated from The Pasadena Playhouse.

Their classmates voted Gene Hackman and Dustin Hoffman "Least Likely To Succeed."

The superstars laugh about it now, but it wasn't funny back then. Few of us have had the success of the two Academy Award winners. However, I'm certain we've had days when we felt nominated for the title of "Least Likely To Succeed."

I love four part harmony. My roots are deep in Southern Gospel Music. My childhood desire was to sing lead for a "name" group. At age 17 I had a stint with The Statesmen. At age 18 I had an equally brief time with The Blackwood Brothers. Heart attacks by vocalists gave me three opportunities of about eight weeks each.

Then my dream job came open as lead singer for Mid-South.

I listed my pastor as a reference. Seeing the manager of the group speaking to my pastor at a concert, I stupidly eavesdropped.

"Malc is a super guy and a real showman, but he is not spiritual and he won't stick with you. He'll be gone before you use all the promo pictures," my pastor said.

I was crushed.

"Least Likely To Succeed" seemed to fit. Yet, in that moment, The Holy Spirit reassured me.

The manager of the group called out to me, "Can we speak?" My heart shouted when he said, "You're our first choice for this position, you were all along. Will you join us?" I lasted five years and four record companies before ending up with Sony. Then I moved on to my true love, pulpit ministry.

> "My thoughts are nothing like your thoughts," says the Lord. "And my ways are far beyond anything you can imagine," (Isaiah 55:8).

For the record, we used up multiple sets of promo pictures.

"Least Likely To Succeed"? That does not describe you.

Act in faith. Schedule your promo pics today.

20
Consider The Consequences

I Tried To Quit A Job.

I had nowhere else to go. Ken Damon was my boss. He helped me learn a lesson. Think things through before acting.

Ken said, "No, you're not quitting. You can't." I started to reply back, but he stopped me cold.

"You have a wife and two children. Where are you going?"

"Your wife just had a child. She can't work. They're depending on you."

Ask Yourself Two Questions:

"What is the best possible outcome?"

"What could be the worst possible outcome?"

In my case there was no good outcome. We had no savings. We had spent everything we had on birthing our new addition. The worst possible outcome was moving in with in-laws and relying on them for everything from housing, to food, to gasoline for the car.

Don't Move Too Quickly.

Do not let anger rule you. It comes at a cost you don't want to pay. Make sure you really do have a clear-cut destination.

> "My dear brothers and sisters, take note of this: Everyone should be quick to listen, slow to speak and slow to become angry, because human anger does not produce the righteousness that God desires," (James 1:19-20 NIV).

I'm a Texan. We are a self-amusing. We are known to laugh at ourselves. Even so, consider a closing bit of wisdom.

> "Saddle Your Hoss Before You Cuss Your Boss,"
> -Texas Proverb.

21
Unintended Consequence

Mr. Majestyk.

A real action movie. I finally saw it recently. I missed it back in 1974. It is pure Charles Bronson. Good versus bad done with attitude.

Something they did not plan became a big deal. They used a 1968 Ford F-150 with no modifications for a number of really extreme stunts. A few years later Ford used several clips from the movie in an advertising campaign called, "Built Ford Tough."

The movie producer did not intend to feature the truck. It was just "one of those things." It just happened. The Ford F-150 became the top-selling vehicle. Over 40 years later, it still is.

Unintended, but real.

Joseph's brothers wronged him. Their jealousy caused them to sell him into slavery. Joseph went through years of isolation and extreme heartache. Then his day of deliverance came and he was promoted to the position as the second most powerful man in the most powerful nation on earth.

In Genesis 50:20 Joseph told his fearful brothers,

> "...You meant it for evil, but God turned it for my good."

Their intention was clearly awful, yet Holy Spirit caused The Law of Unintended Consequence to manifest in Joseph's favor.

Let your imagination soar. Dream. God, in His goodness, is turning things around for you. Get ready for better. God desires to make you the F-150 of today.

Everything you need is already in your life. Believe it. Look for it. Embrace it.

God is turning it for your good!

22
More Awful News

Broke.

Pressured.

Call it what you will.

The US Commerce Department says only about 50% of US Citizens could write a $500 check today. The rest would see their need go unmet, or they would be forced to rely on credit cards.

I'm not in that spot. No, I'm not "rolling in dough." But, I'm not in "that" place today. Honestly, I'd heard a similar report last year. It moved me to decide to gather protection against life's storms.

The world has never needed the message of God's desire for our prosperity more than today.

> "Beloved, I wish above all things that you may prosper and be in good health, even as your soul prospers," (3 John 2).

Man is a tripartite being. We are composed of body, soul and spirit. In the verse above, John expresses the desire of our Lord that we prosper in every area of our lives: in our health, in our spirit, and soul (thought life).

Man has needs in three areas: The physical, spiritual, and financial realms.

No Christian doubts Jesus is our Savior. Far too few believe He heals. Too many doubt He blesses. I believe all three promises. So, I'm living in the victory today that is produced by this ongoing decision.

I'll make the decision to believe and live there again tomorrow, too.

23
Three Thoughts About Words

Words Are Incredible.

They can give life, or they can kill. Words spoken by a leader can start a war. Words spoken by that same leader can stop a war. Consider these three powerful truths about words:

Words Create A Climate That Supports Success or Failure

> *"You will have to live with the consequences of everything you say, "(Proverbs 18:20, Good News Translation).*

I have spoken sharply and wounded someone I loved. I tried to "take it back", but the damage was already done. Solomon was right: I had to live with the results my words had created.

Words Produce Passion, Power or Poison

> *"Words kill, words give life; they are either poison or fruit - you choose, "(Proverbs 18:21 The Message Bible).*

Words can inject life into a relationship. Words spoken by that same person can inject poison. It is easier to not speak poison than to use words as an antidote.

Words Can Transform Your Life Into a Success Zone

> *"Make your words good; you'll be glad you did,"* (Proverbs 18:20 Contemporary English Version).

This is a question I ask often. Please ponder it: What are you saying about your life? What are you saying about your job, friendships, or marriage? Are you speaking words of affirmation and blessing over your children?

Are you declaring the prosperity of God over your family, employer, and your home church?

Death and life really are in the power of the tongue.

I've learned something the hard way; I may not love the fruit created by my words, but I will have to eat it.

24

Silencing The Haters

King Balak.

Prophet Balaam.

Balak hated Israel. Balaam loved money. Balaam was more sorcerer than prophet.

God told Joshua, "No man shall stand before you." Yet, here we see King Balak trying to resist Israel's march to the Promised Land by using Balaam's skills.

We can learn a valuable blessing from the life of Balaam. Repeated sacrifices and attempts to undo Israel caused him to conclude,

> *"How can I curse what God has chosen to bless?"*
> *(Numbers 23:8).*

There is plenty of deep theology here. But I'm happy to simply use this as simple encouragement. Almost all who read this have had episodes of criticism directed your way. In my case I've endured the pain produced by the opinions and chosen to walk on in faith. Balaam learned he could not really curse Israel and stop their Kingdom momentum. However, at Baal Peor he hit on a destructive key: distract the people with temptation and move them away from the favor of God.

I am living in great favor today. But I've tasted the fruit of a Baal Peor distraction. No, I didn't go into paganism and turn away from God. I lost my focus.

I have already entered my Promised Land. My goal is to take more territory every day I live.

There are times when memories of hateful words rise. During those rough moments I silence the voice of the enemy through spoken words of faith. I encourage you to do the same thing.

What are you saying about you? That is what really matters.

> *"Blessed be everyone who blesses you, and cursed be everyone who curses you," (Numbers 24:9b).*

Only two opinions matter today: Your chosen focus and the direction of God. As a believer you're already in your personal Promised Land. Instead of allowing yourself to be tormented by the past, explore the blessings of God today.

25
Thoughts on Destiny

We all have a destiny.

It will be driven by a "God Dream." Or, it will be directed by human desires. It could also be a path steered by demonic influence.

Movies, Plays, The Bible

I like movies.

"I Am Your Father, Luke,"—Darth Vader.

The Star Wars Series sent Luke in a pretty good direction. His father, Lord Vader, was a good guy gone wrong…to the dark side. Luke could have seen his destiny as being the same as that of his father. Instead, he chose a better way. He embraced the higher pathway taught by Obi Wan Kenobi.

An Ancient Play

Euripides wrote the original Hercules play. Seneca came along with what we call a sequel, *"No Man Escapes His Fate, Hercules." "The Madness Of Hercules"* continued the "franchise" in 54 AD. This play presents Hercules as having an inescapably harsh destiny.

A Much Better Way to Live

"I Know The Plans I Have For You, Thoughts of Good and Not of Evil," —The Lord, (Jeremiah 29:11A).

God has a good plan for everyone. If your upbringing was rotten, life today doesn't have to be. You are not predestined to a life of failure. God's plan for you is a good one. Seek it out, live it out.

Make high quality decisions on a daily basis.

Let me share two of my declarations of faith in closing this chapter:

> *Faith Will Govern My Life, Not Emotions.*

> *Yet, I Will Deliberately Manifest Two Emotions Daily: Thanksgiving and Compassion.*

26
My First Valentine

I Was Crazy About Her.

I had no idea how to let her know. Then came Valentine's Day and the answer. Mom bought me a box of 100 Valentine's Day Cards. After great thought, I addressed 30 cards to my love interest. Soon she stood before my classroom desk with the pile of cards held tightly in her hands. She gave me a penetrating look, then a soft smile, and said, "You're weird."

Shortly thereafter we planned our wedding. We didn't want to rush into things, so we agreed to wait until we were 10. Sadly, she moved away during the summer between grades two and three...*never to be seen again.*

Saint Valentine was a real person.

A Roman Emperor needed highly focused soldiers. So, he declared marriage illegal for young men. As a priest, Father Valentine opposed the policy and conducted secret weddings. Later on he rescued Christian soldiers from Roman jail. Eventually Father Valentine was arrested and imprisoned.

A young woman visited to feed and pray with Valentine. The two fell in love and communicated by mail. The smitten man signed, "Your Valentine." A tradition was birthed.

From Mt. Calvary Jesus wrote humanity a love letter. The message was "Written in Red." It can be easily understood. Whosoever will may read.

Happy Valentine's Day!

Every day...*today!*

27
You Can't Advance Beyond Your Faith

Faith is ever increasing. Or, it is shrinking by lack of use. Faith is built-or destroyed-by what we do daily.

We are defined, blessed and promoted by our difference.

Defined By Faith

Moses was defined by faith. He was brought out of Egyptian bondage through believing faith. His leadership became memorably established because he allowed faith to define his life.

Inexplicably Blessed by Faith

Jonah was blessed by the inexplicable goodness of God. Faith caused Jonah to repent in view of his belief God is good. Tossed overboard because of sin, Jonah was rescued in an unusual way by being swallowed by a huge fish managed to save his life.

Promoted By Faith

People of active faith sense and pursue their destiny. Faith thinks through and produces belief systems. Valid belief systems produce a legacy of faith.

A legacy of faith yields generational blessing. Your efforts today are making a difference. Release your faith to create things.

Be bold. Enjoy being different. You'll find it's a good thing.

28
An Early Church Miracle

This Is A Powerful Story.

A crippled man begged by the street. He was outside the Beautiful Gate in Jerusalem. Peter and John, freshly filled with the Holy Spirit, were on their way to morning worship. They had probably walked past this man hundreds of times. But on this particular day, they saw him and he listened to them.

Peter commanded, "In The Name of Jesus of Nazareth, rise up and walk..." and He did. The lame man was miraculously healed, and his story became the hottest news in the big city. Some could not grasp how it happened. Apostle Peter could not fathom the idea of people in Jerusalem who didn't know of the greatness of Jesus.

"The Big Fisherman" took the moment to explain how this thing had transpired.

Peter said,

> "And His Name, through faith in His Name, has made this man whole..." (Acts 3:16).

7 Facts About The Name of Jesus

1. We can't separate the person from The Name.

2. Calling The Name is the first step to accessing the person.

3. Jesus is the giver of our faith.

4. Jesus is the object of our faith.

5. We can't just say *"...in The Name of Jesus."* We must have faith in, be firmly convinced of, the power inherent within the Name of Jesus.

6. We believe *before* we see.

7. We see *after* we say.

We rule and reign here on earth.

Agents can act in the name of who they represent.

This reign is not in our name, but in the Name of Jesus.

We can expect powerful results each time we use that Name!

29
I Hate Religion

Religion is knowing about God.

Relationship is knowing God personally.

Religion likes everything to be nice and tidy. Religion prefers the hurting to suffer in silence. Religion would rather have you live in the fog of pain medicines rather than become a "faith-filled fanatic" who is constantly seeking your miracle.

Relationship caused blind Bartimaeus to scream out to The Healer, "Jesus, Son of David, have mercy on me!" He upset the religious. But he received his eyesight. Religion will keep you living in mercy. Relationship will compel you to live in the fullness of grace.

Effort matters in The Kingdom. Thank God for the example of Bartimaeus (Mark 10:46-52).

> "Sadly, those living outside the realm of active faith often believe everything that happens to them, good or bad, is the will of God," -Malcolm Burton. Excerpt from "Miracles: In Black and White."

Press into relationship today. Trust me, you will not miss religion.

As we said in Plum Grove, "Not for a single, solitary minute."

30
I Don't Want to Forget

"Remind me," I said.

"No, I won't do that," she replied. "Needing to remind you means it doesn't matter to you."

"Actually, needing a reminder only means I'm human...*and I can forget things*," I replied.

Ask me. It's ok.

"What have you forgotten, Malc?"

Honestly, I've forgotten too many things. Birthdays? (Ugh... *once*). Professional appointments? Yes. Due dates on important bills? Uh huh.

Yet, there is something I'm determined to remember.

> *"Remember the wonders He has done, His miracles..."*
> *(Joshua 3:14).*

I've been well-treated. So, I work hard at remembering my family and friends. And I'm determined not to forget Him...*not for a single moment.*

31
Prospecting

Prospecting is part of sales. Each prospect is a potential sale. Each prospect then must be qualified. The sales professional discerns willingness and ability. The person who is willing and able to buy is a true prospect.

My ministry colleagues know I hold John Wesley in very high esteem. His theology is, essentially, my theology. It is heavy on grace without robbing God of His sovereignty.

An Interesting Approach

Wesley's approach was always interesting. His preaching involved simultaneous prospecting. Wesley was known to seek out candidates for salvation and ministry in the same service.

> *"Those of you who feel destined for hell can just as easily be reconciled to God, and do the work of the ministry. Won't you receive His saving work, and His call to ministry in this moment?" ---John Wesley.*

Wesley Did Three Unique Things

Convention did not stop Wesley. He instituted things we still benefit from.

1. Wesley Originated What We Now Call Small Groups.

Pastors were in short supply. Back then a theology degree was required. Revival was burning so brightly preachers were in short supply. As a result of this Wesley developed a method for small meetings. There will always be detractors. The Church of England disdained Wesley's results. Too many were claiming to be born again.

They said God was not in it. Wesley was just "working a system." His followers and ministers were "...just a bunch of Methodists."

2. Wesley Ordained Pastors Who Were Not Seminary Graduates.

Tom Pate was an exceptional Evangelist. He had a powerful impact on me when I was young. He had played second base for the St. Louis Cardinals. He didn't get to play much because was a backup to Hall of Farmer Red Schoendienst.

Tom said something both funny and profound, "I don't know the difference between hermeneutics and eschatology, but I understand the Word of God and the anointing that is required to preach it."

Wesley would have understood Tom's way of thinking. He would also have approved of Tom's way of thinking.

3. Wesley Ordained Women To Preach The Word of God

One of my daughters serves as an ordained minister. I'm not in favor of her ministry because she's my girl. No, it is because she has demonstrated God's call. What original thing is God calling you to do?

I'm determined to remain open to "new".

Great things lie ahead!

www.ingramcontent.com/pod-product-compliance
Lightning Source LLC
LaVergne TN
LVHW051157080426
835508LV00021B/2673